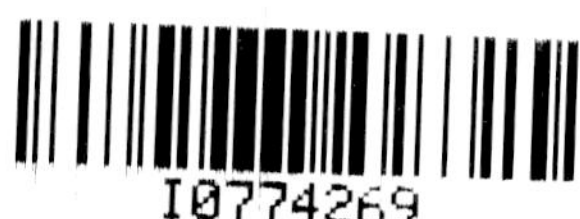

With gratitude to God for all blessings, and unconditional love to my dear family.
You are my greatest treasure.

Bruno Gomes
2024

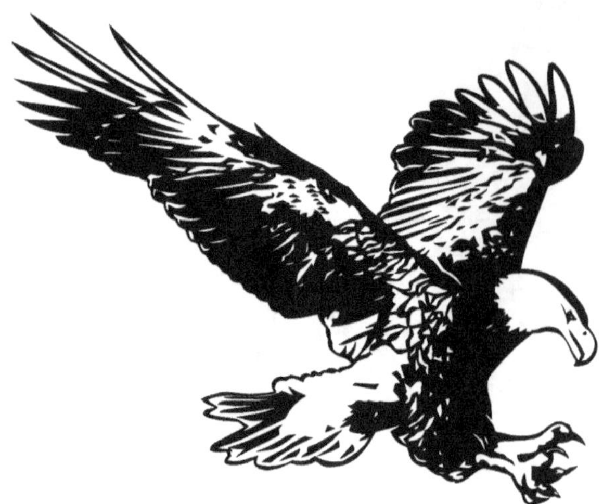

This Book Belongs to:

____

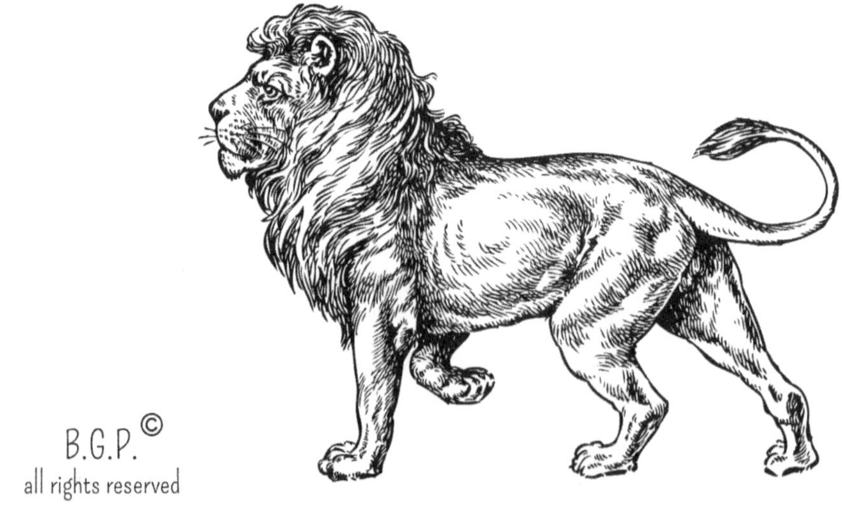

Test Color Page

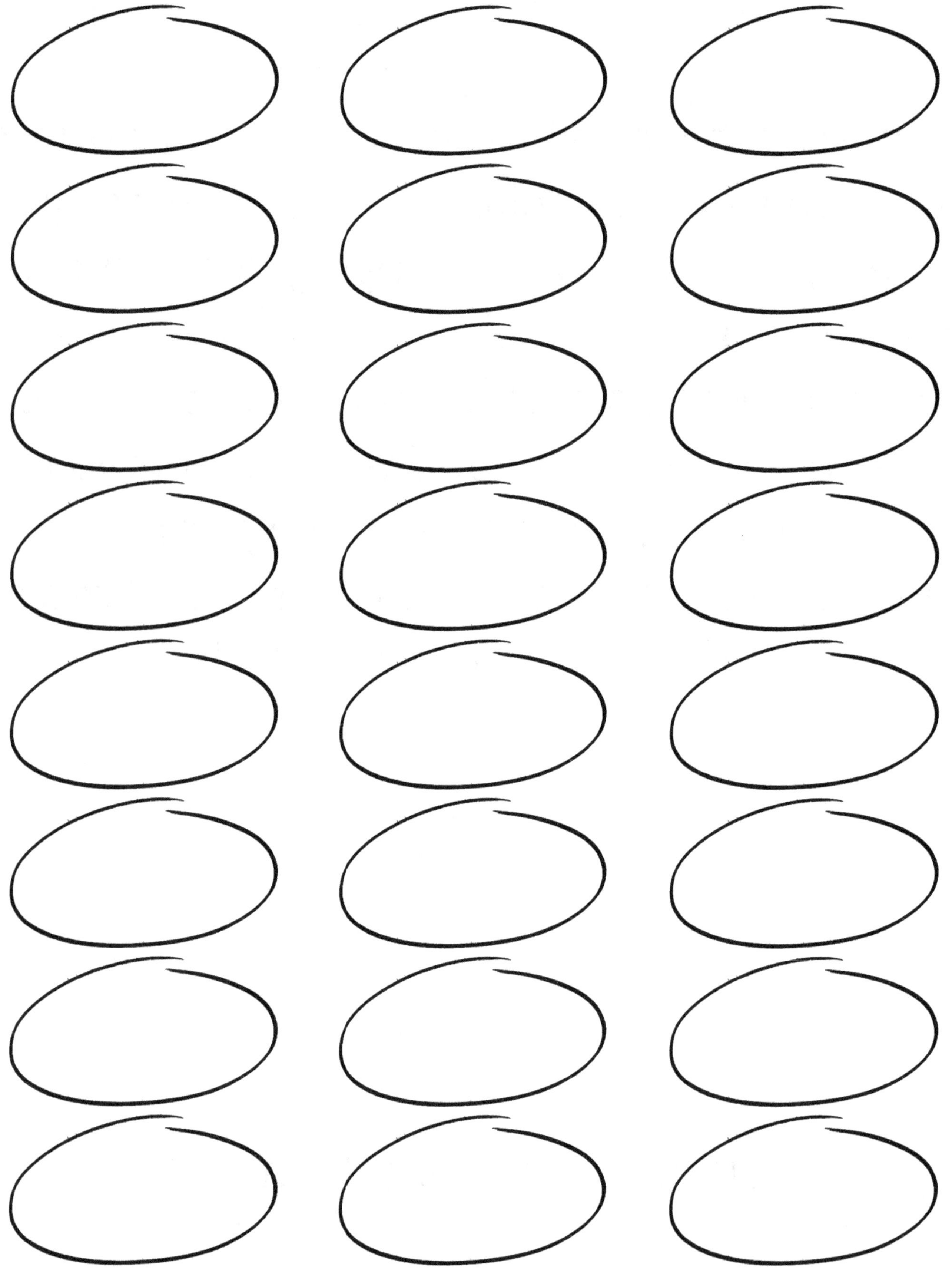

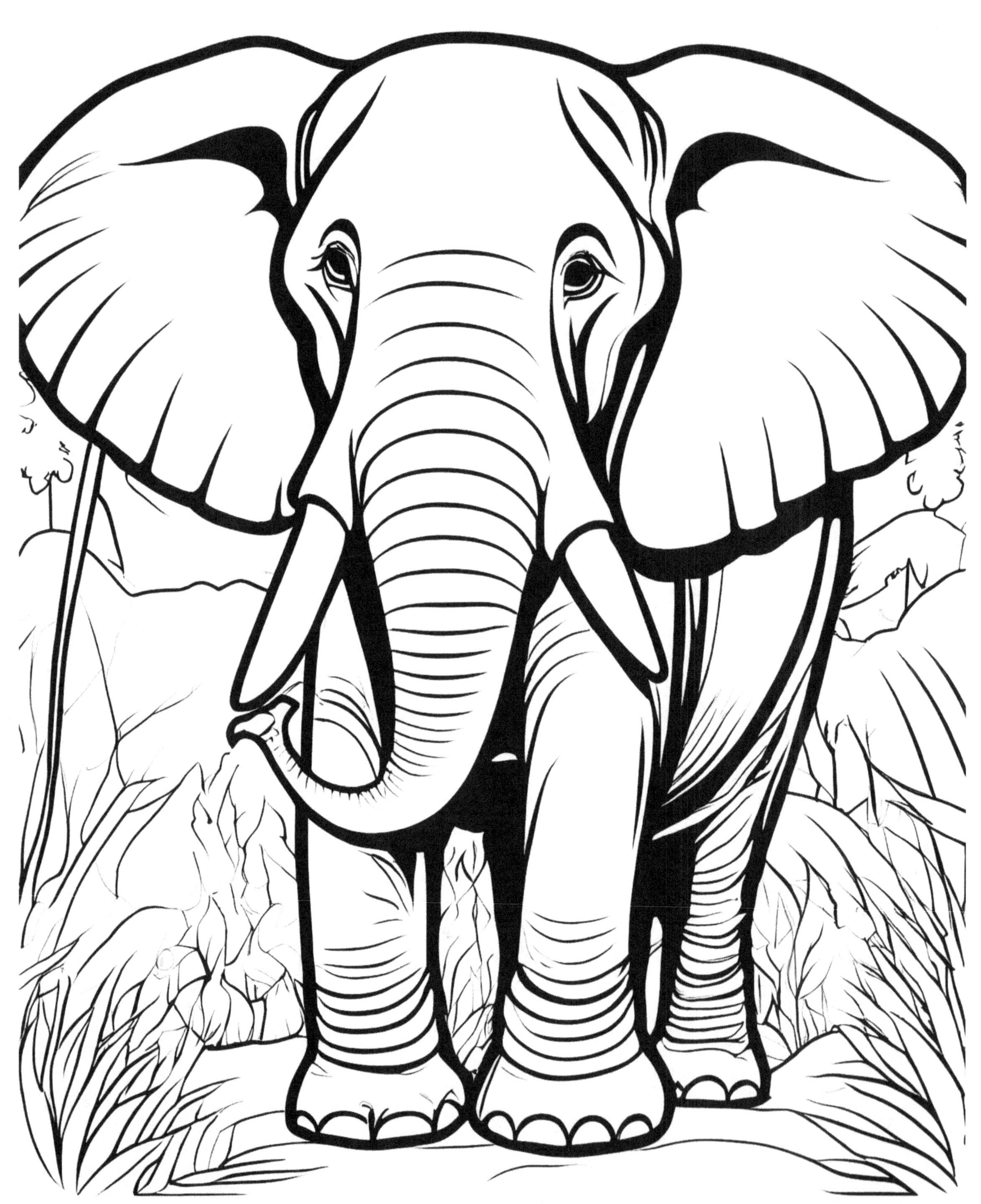

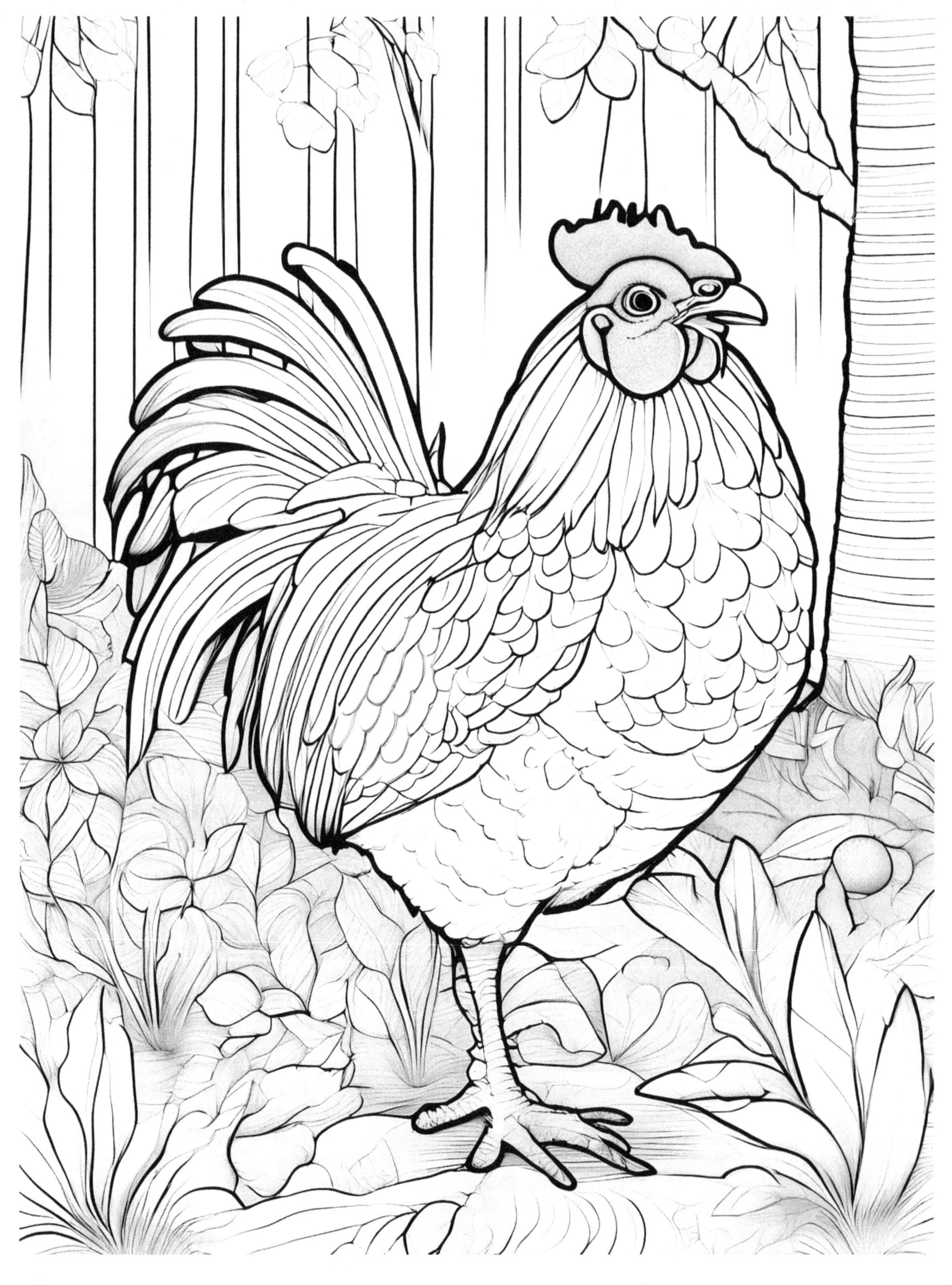

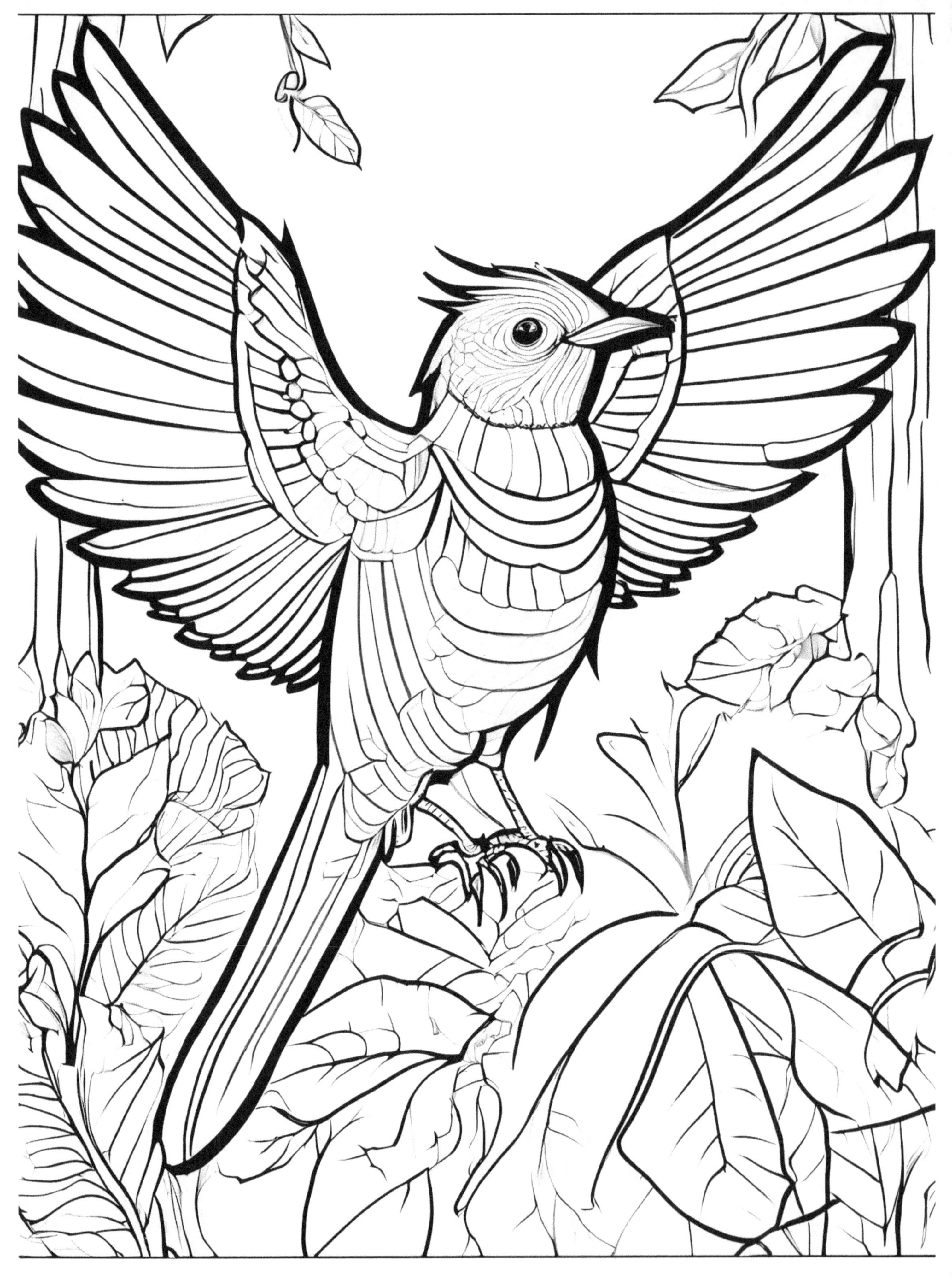

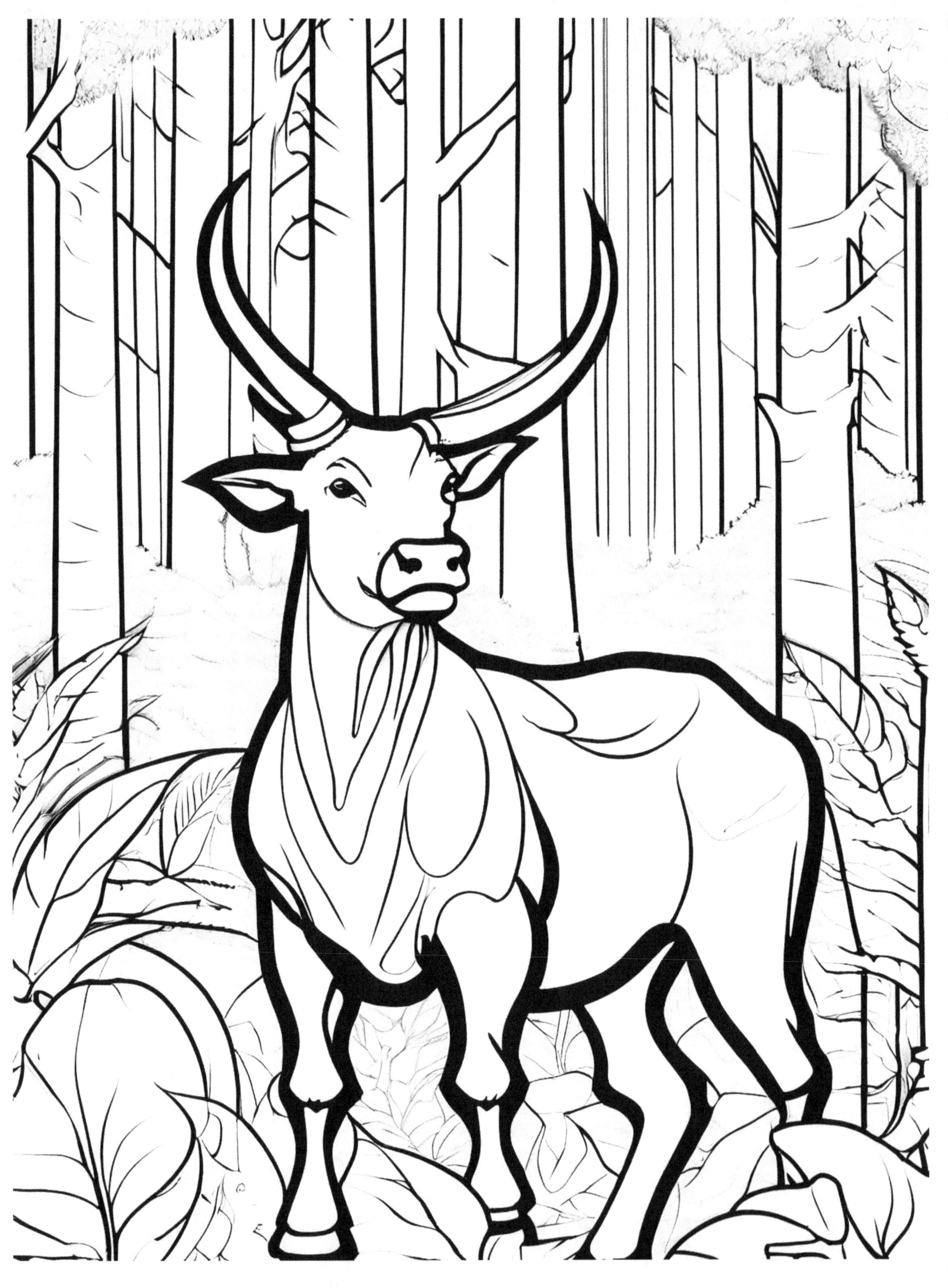

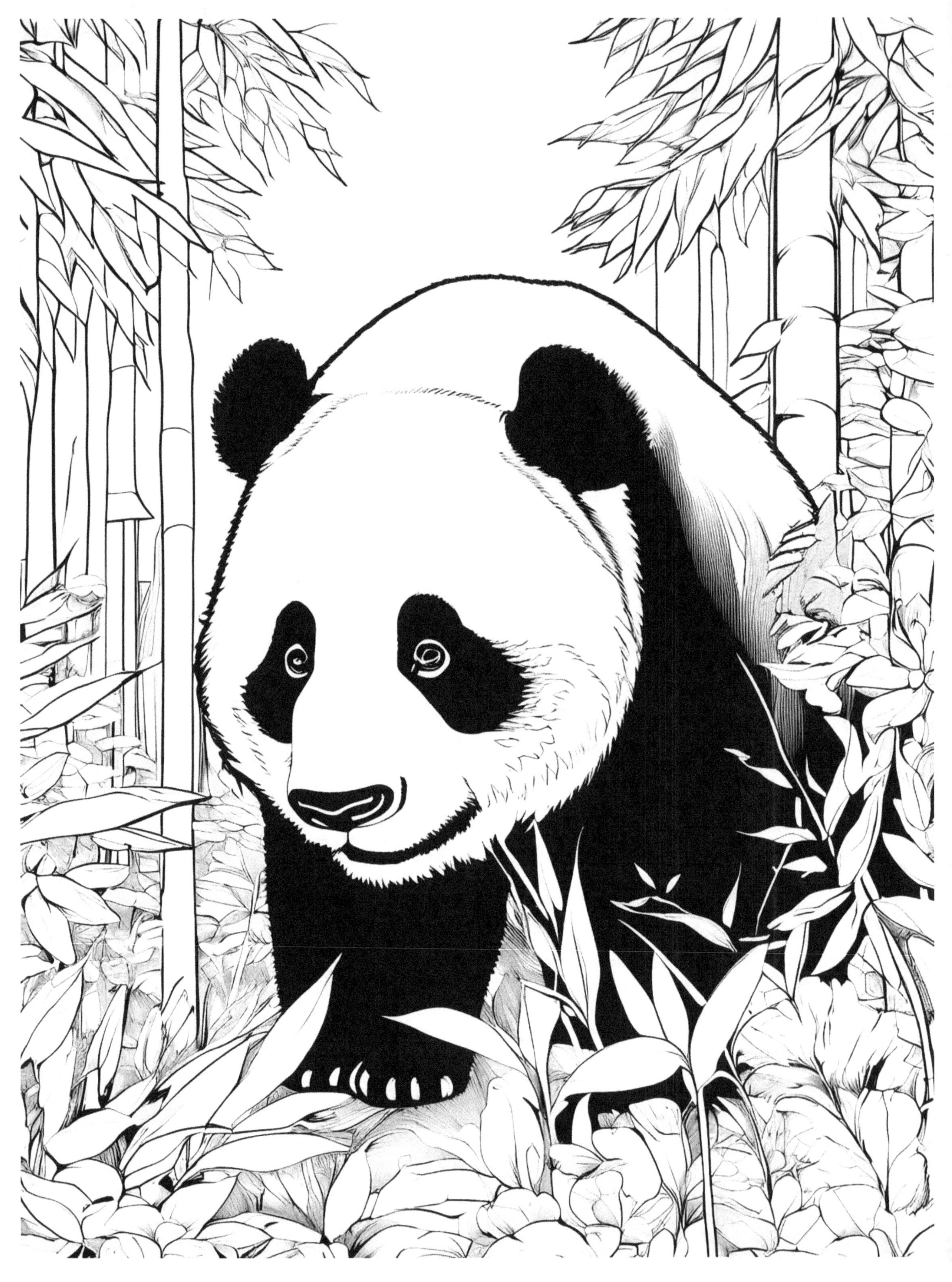

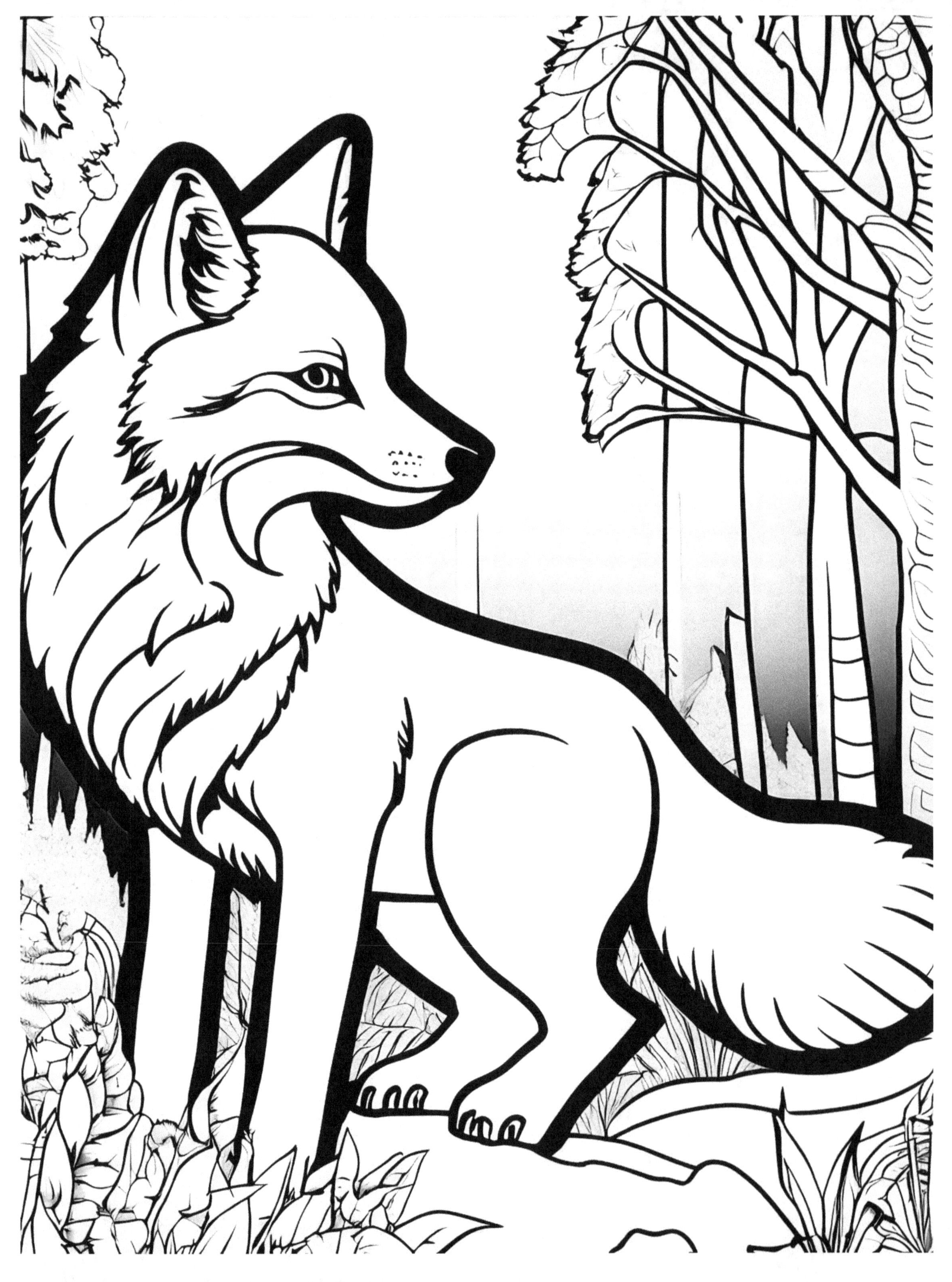

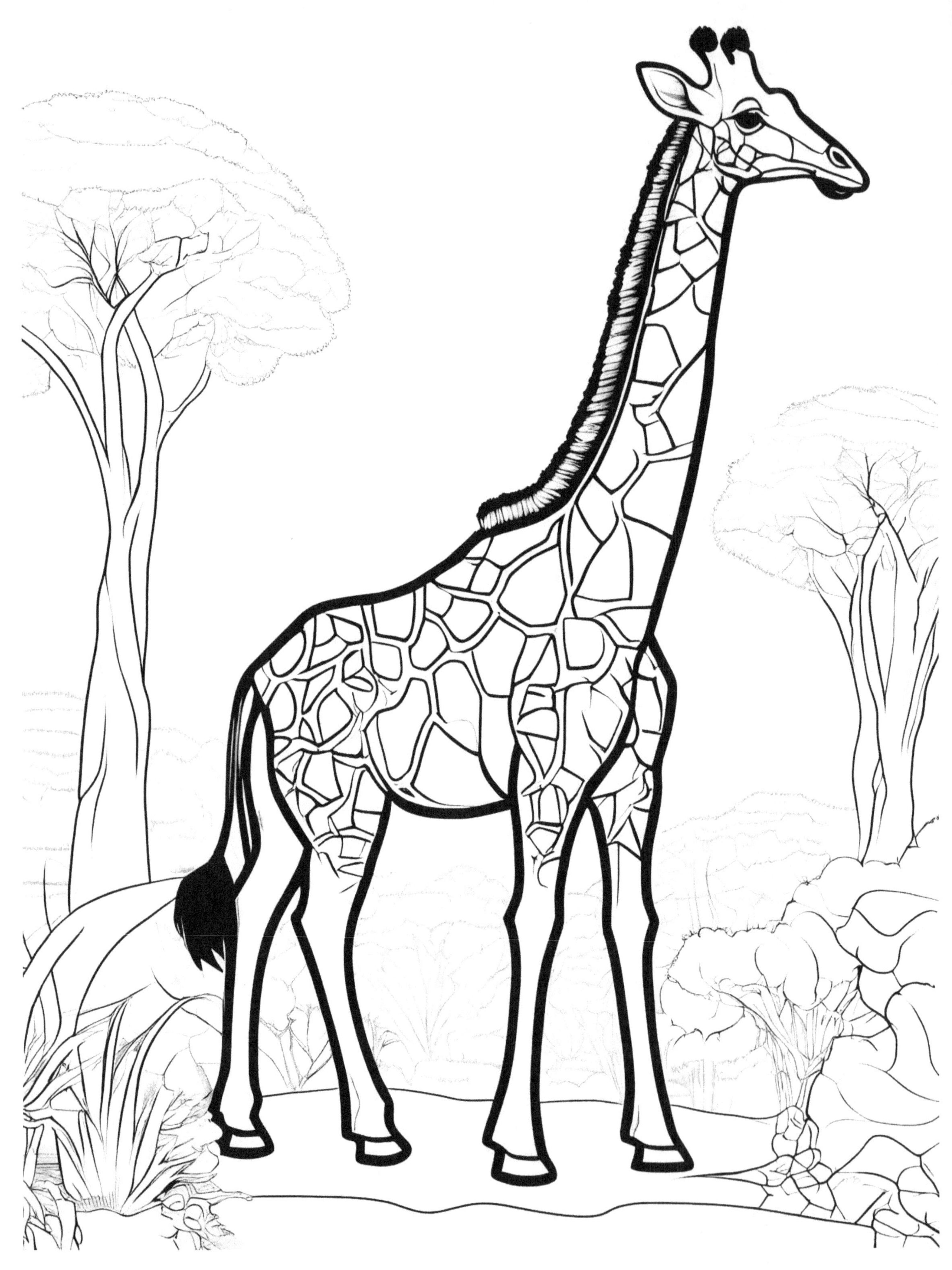

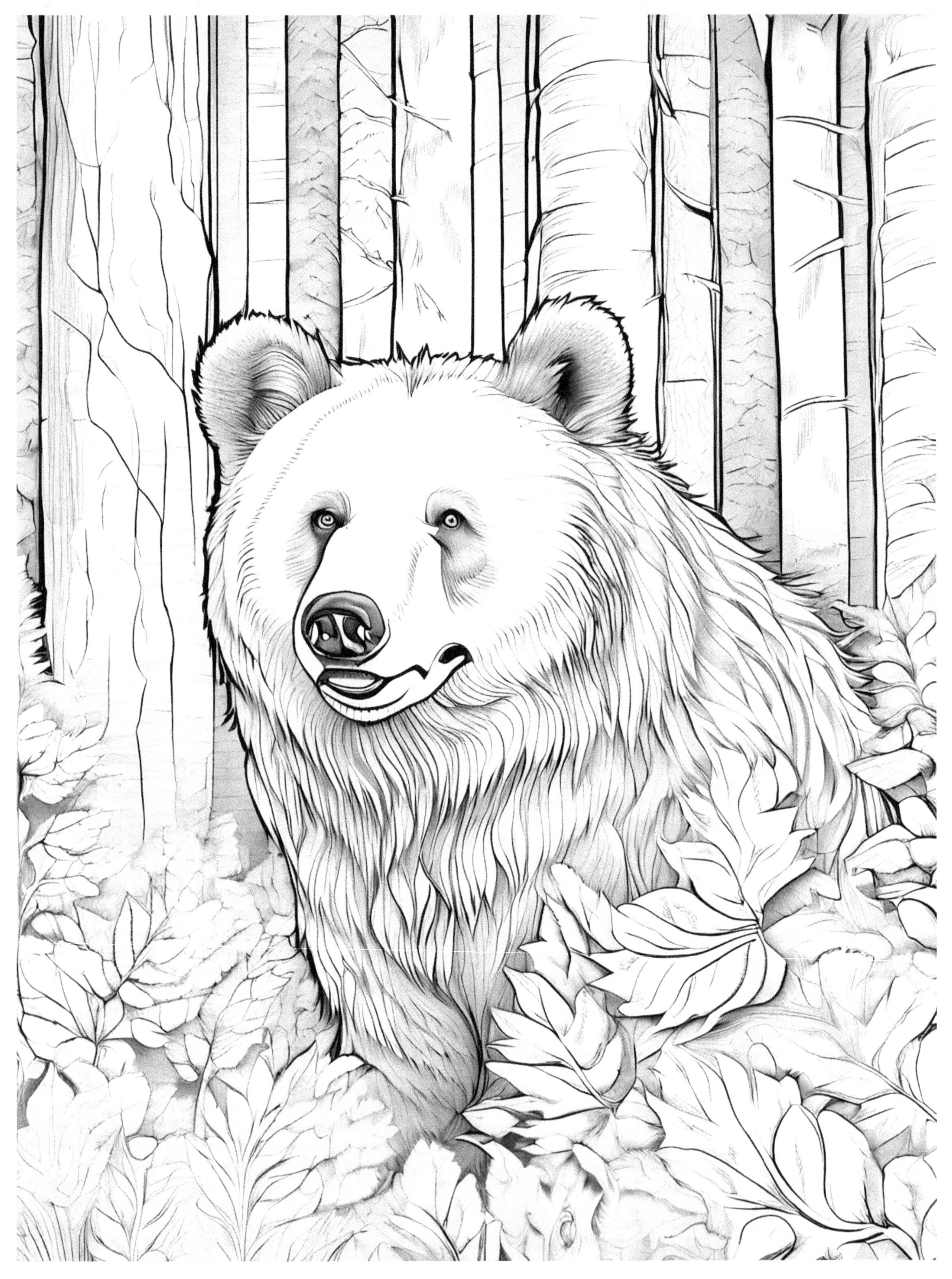

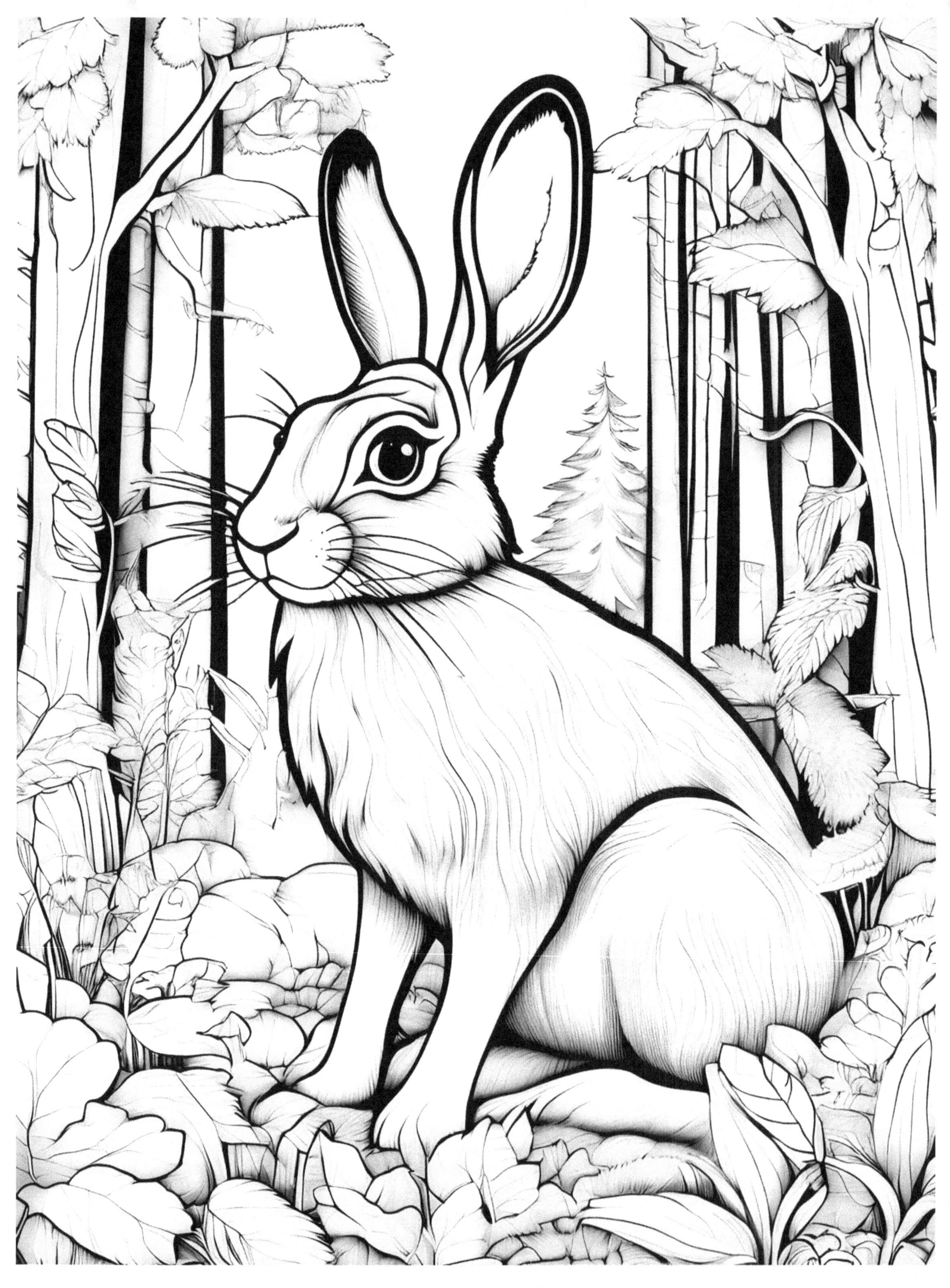

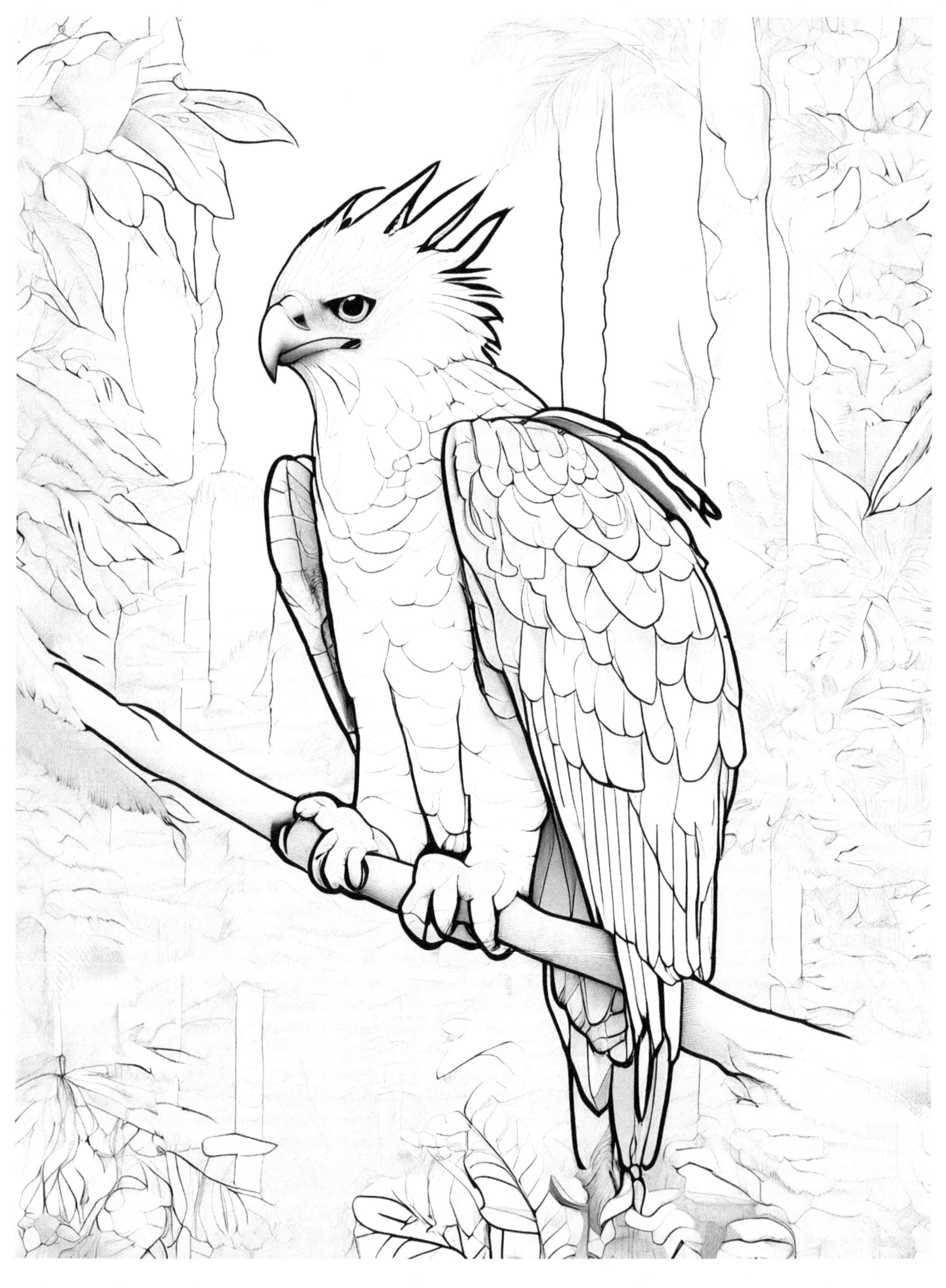

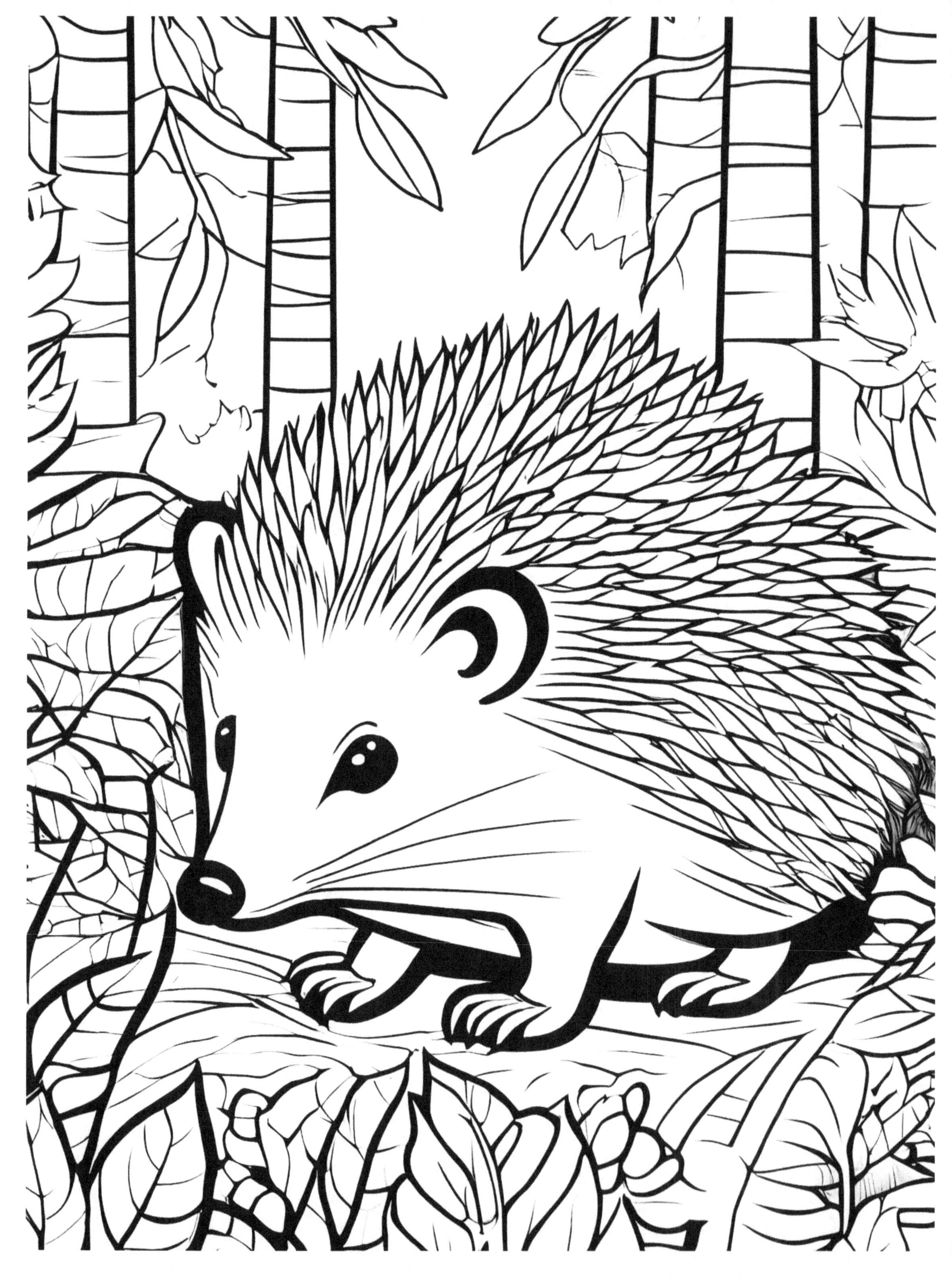

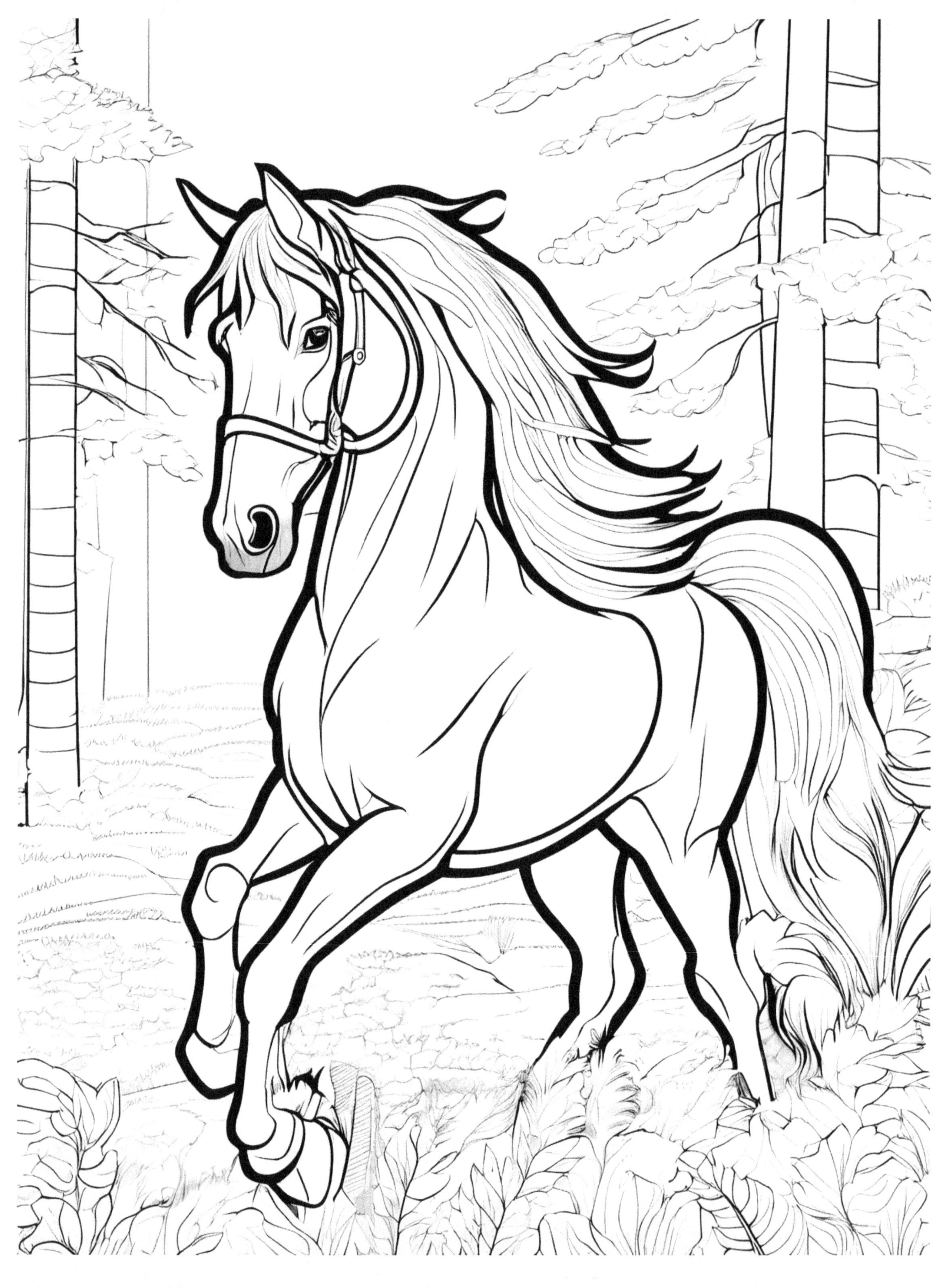

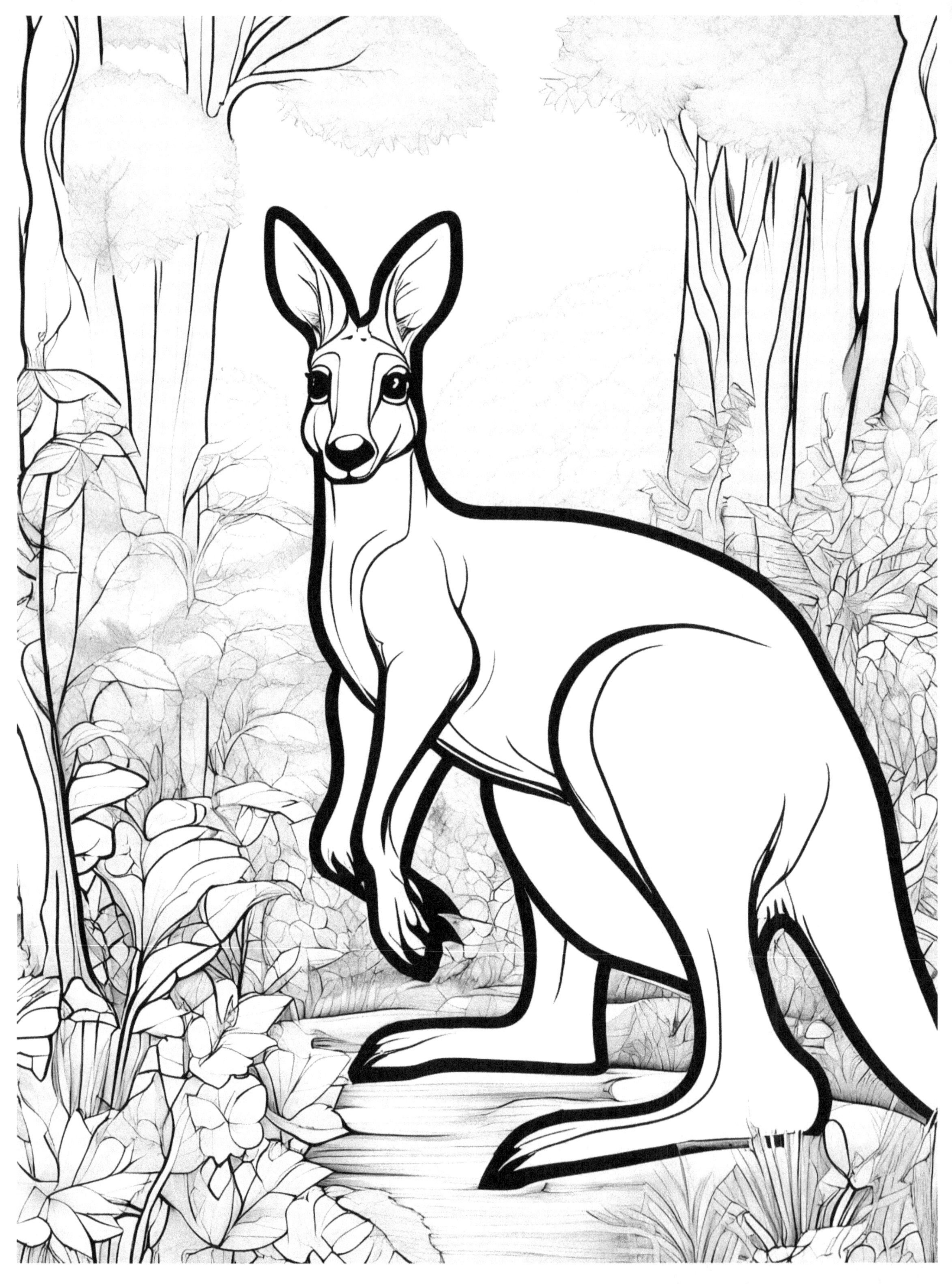

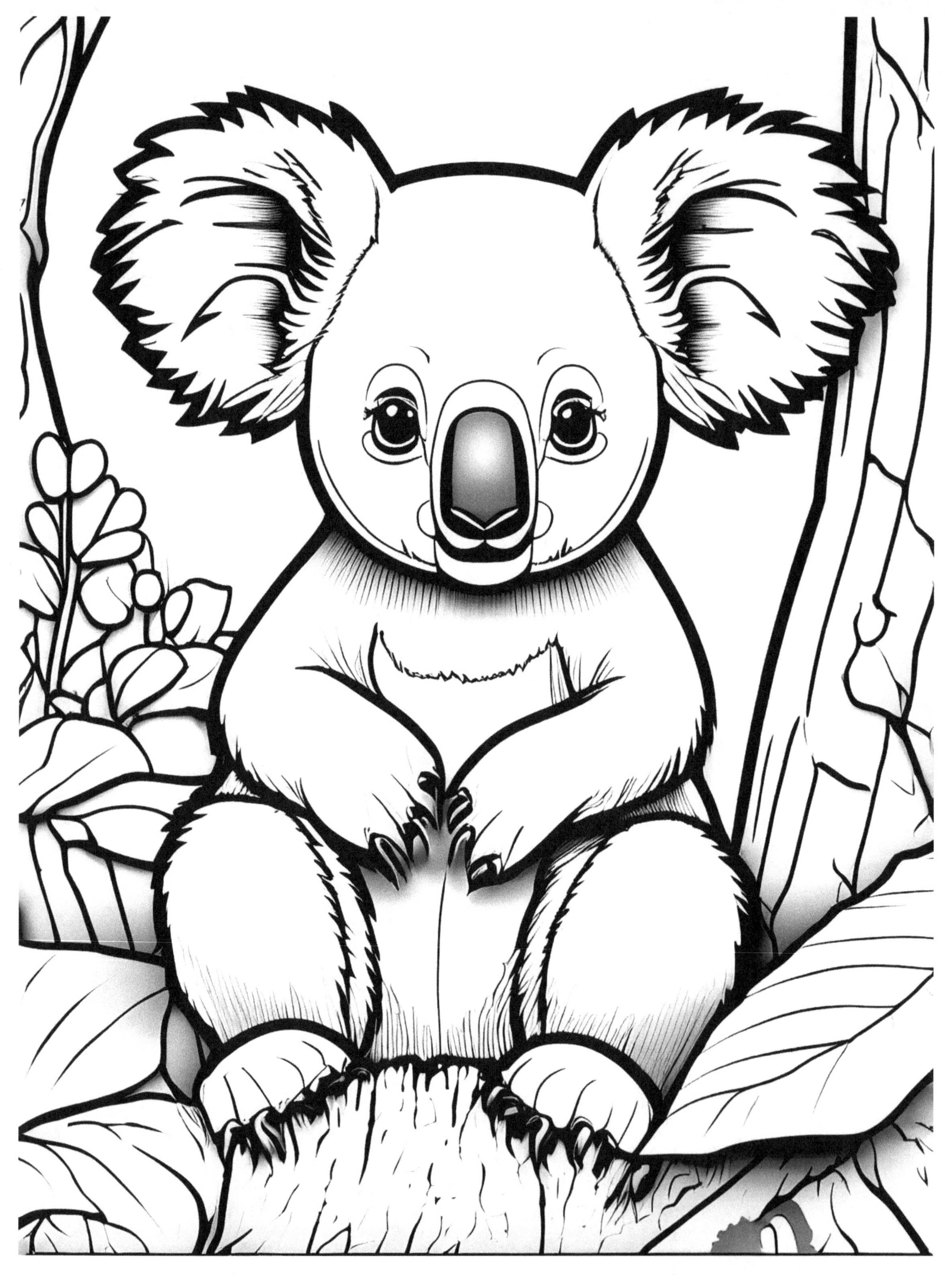

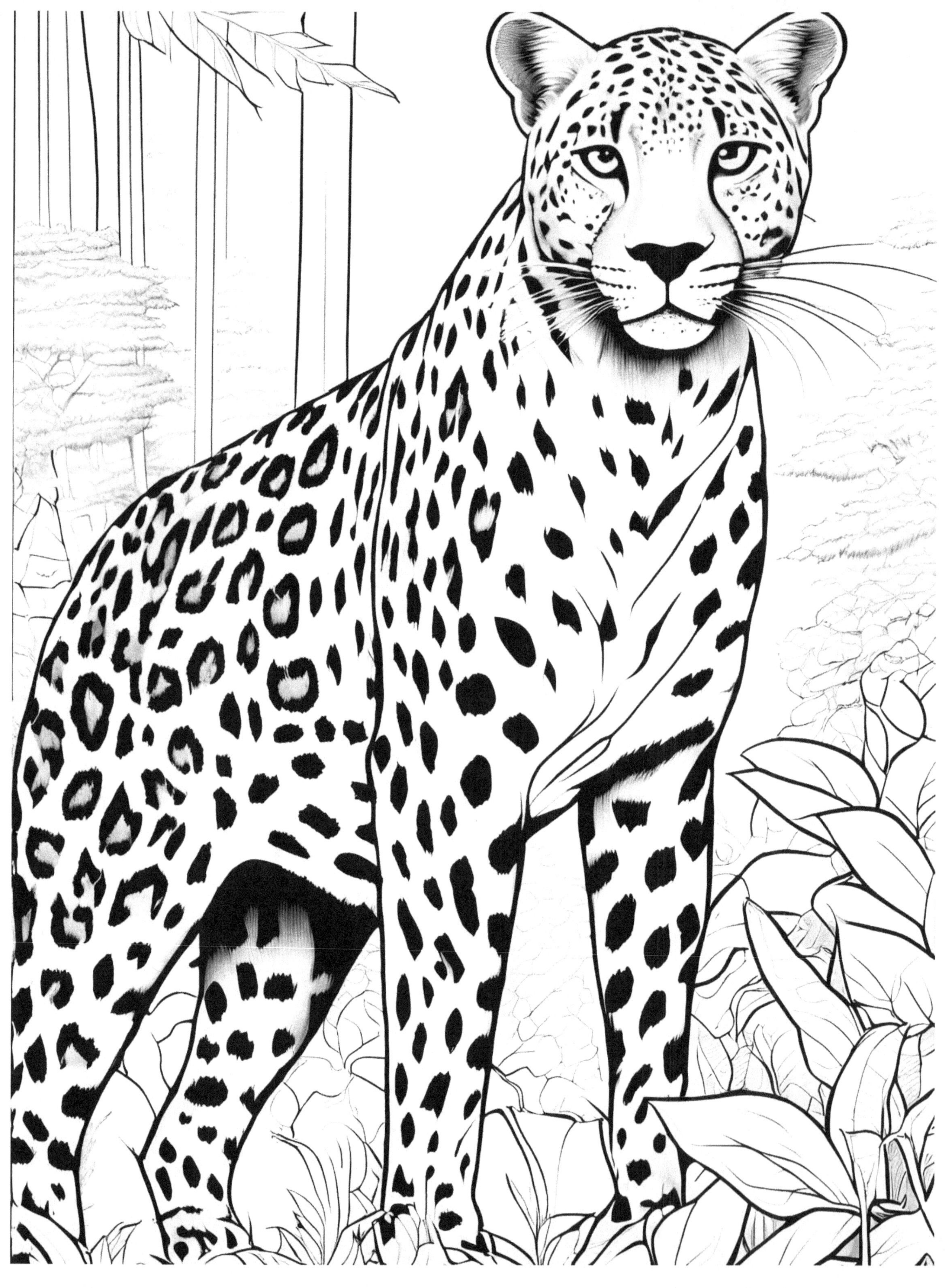

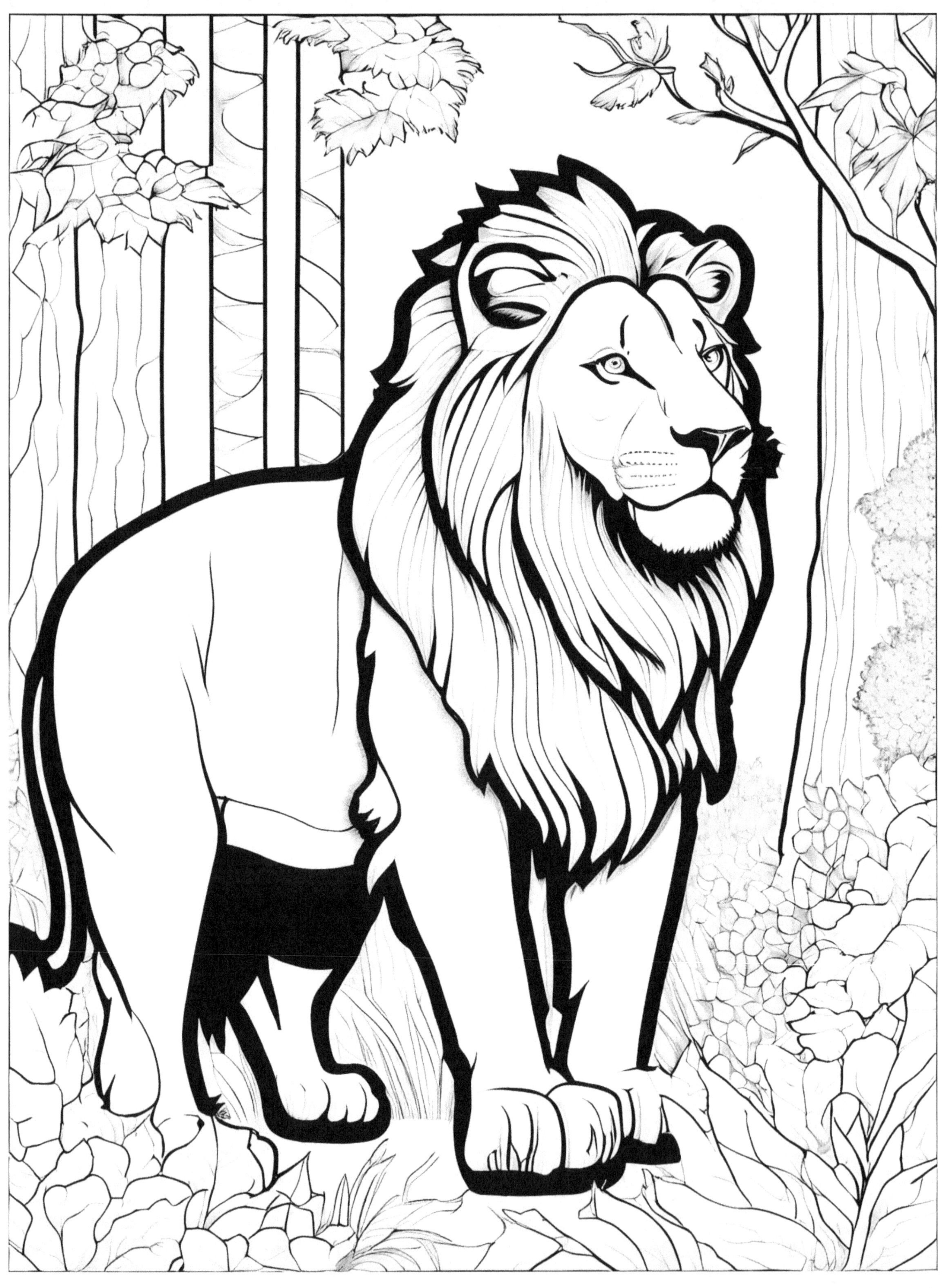

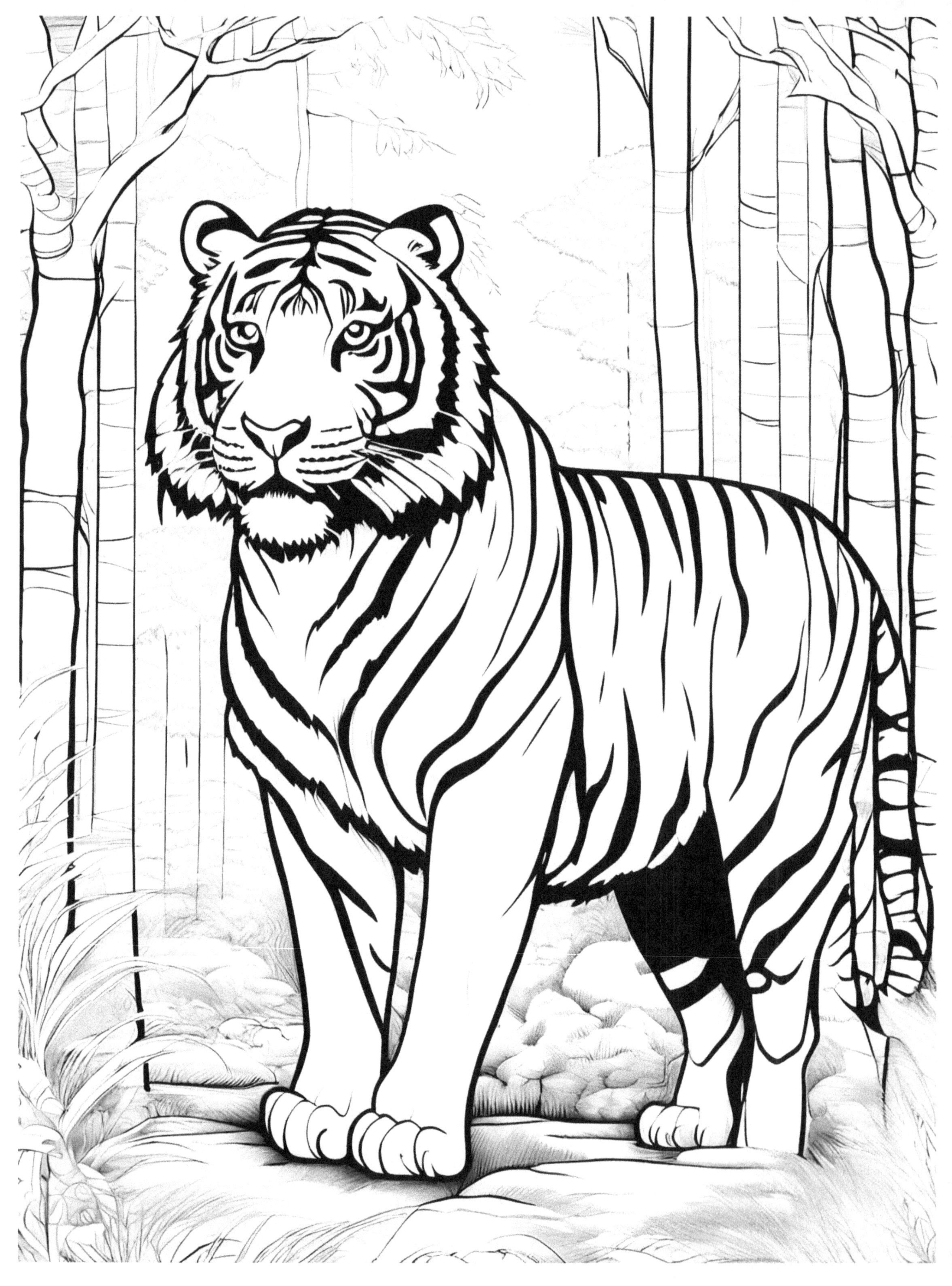

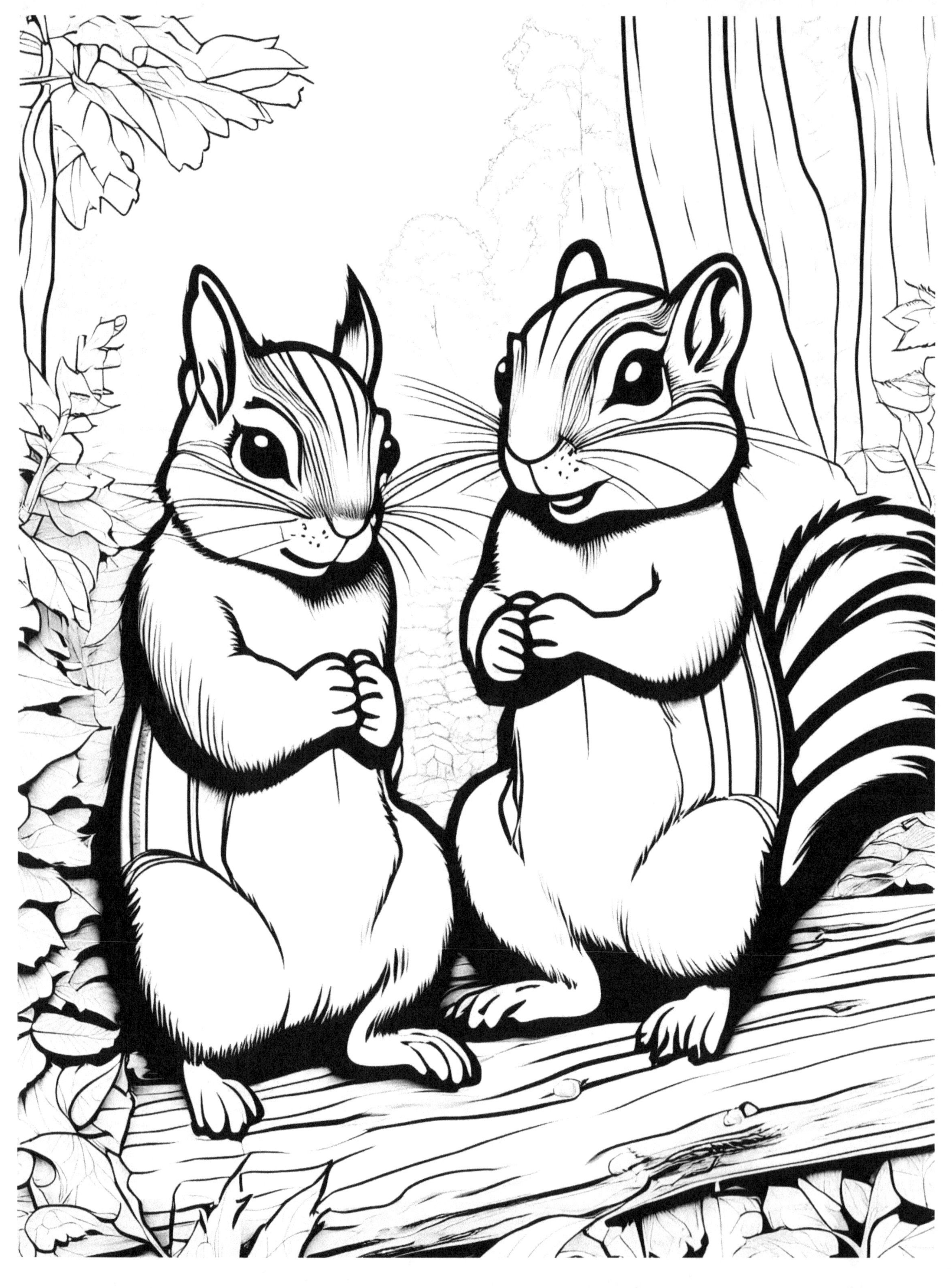

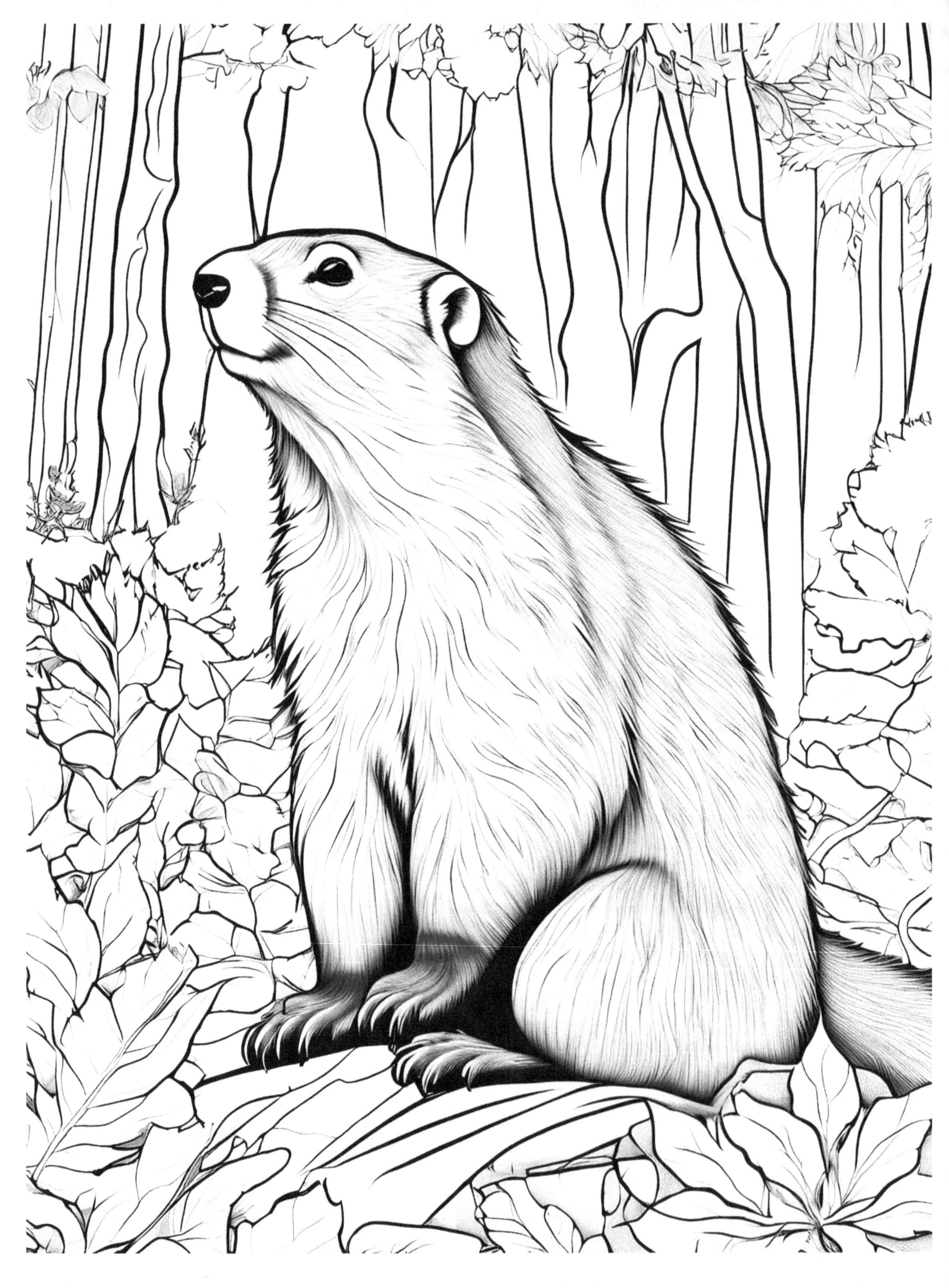

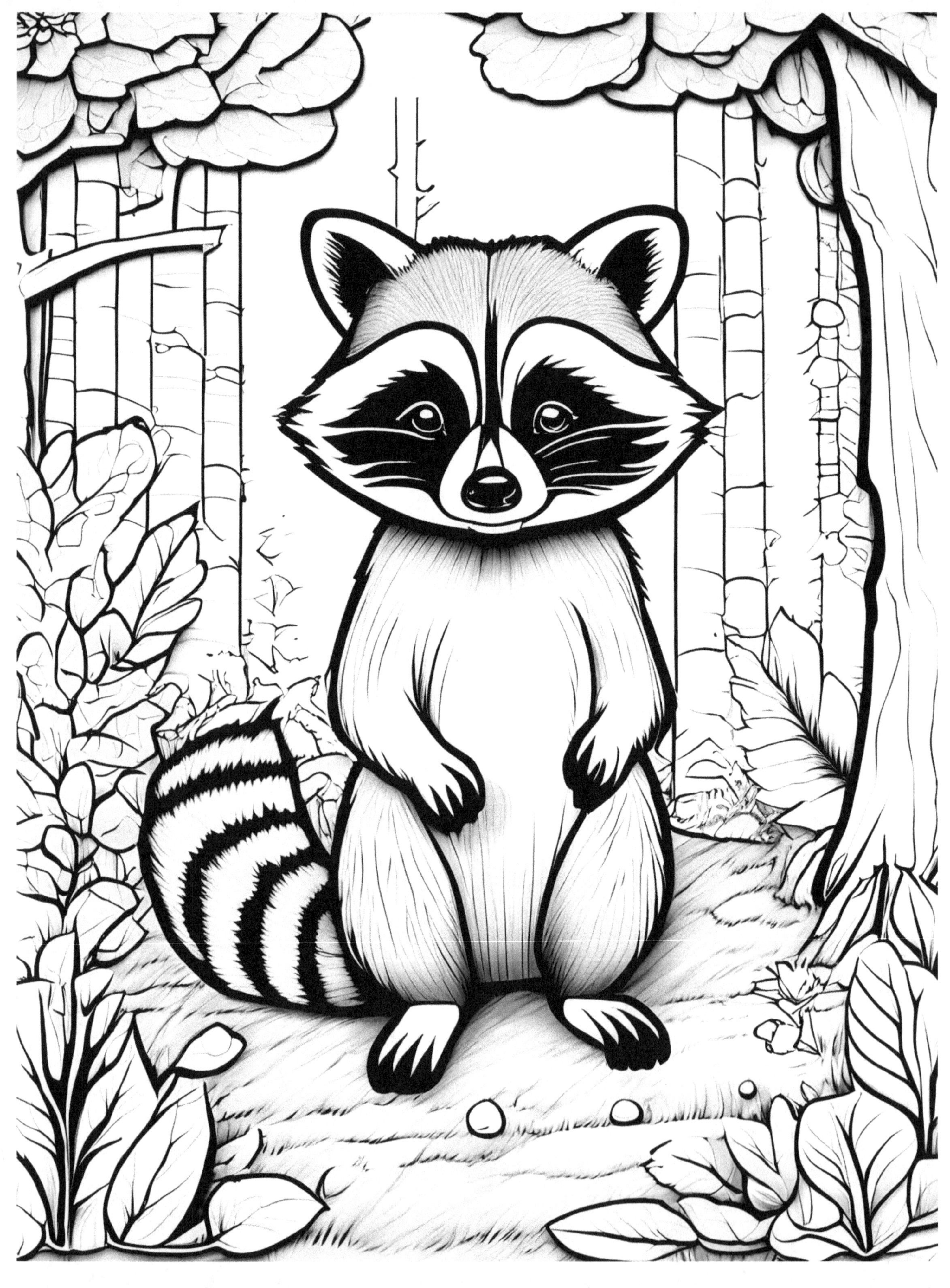

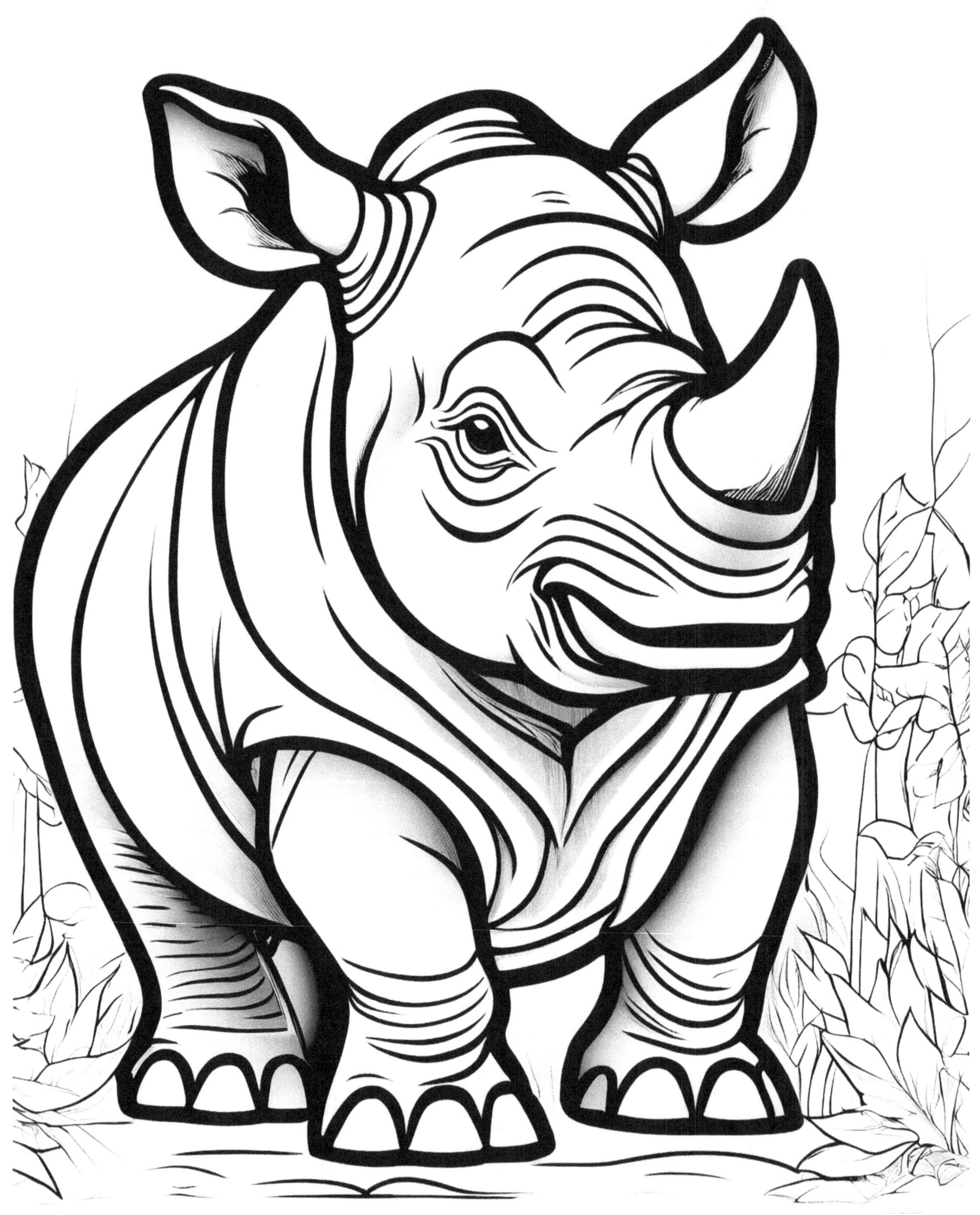

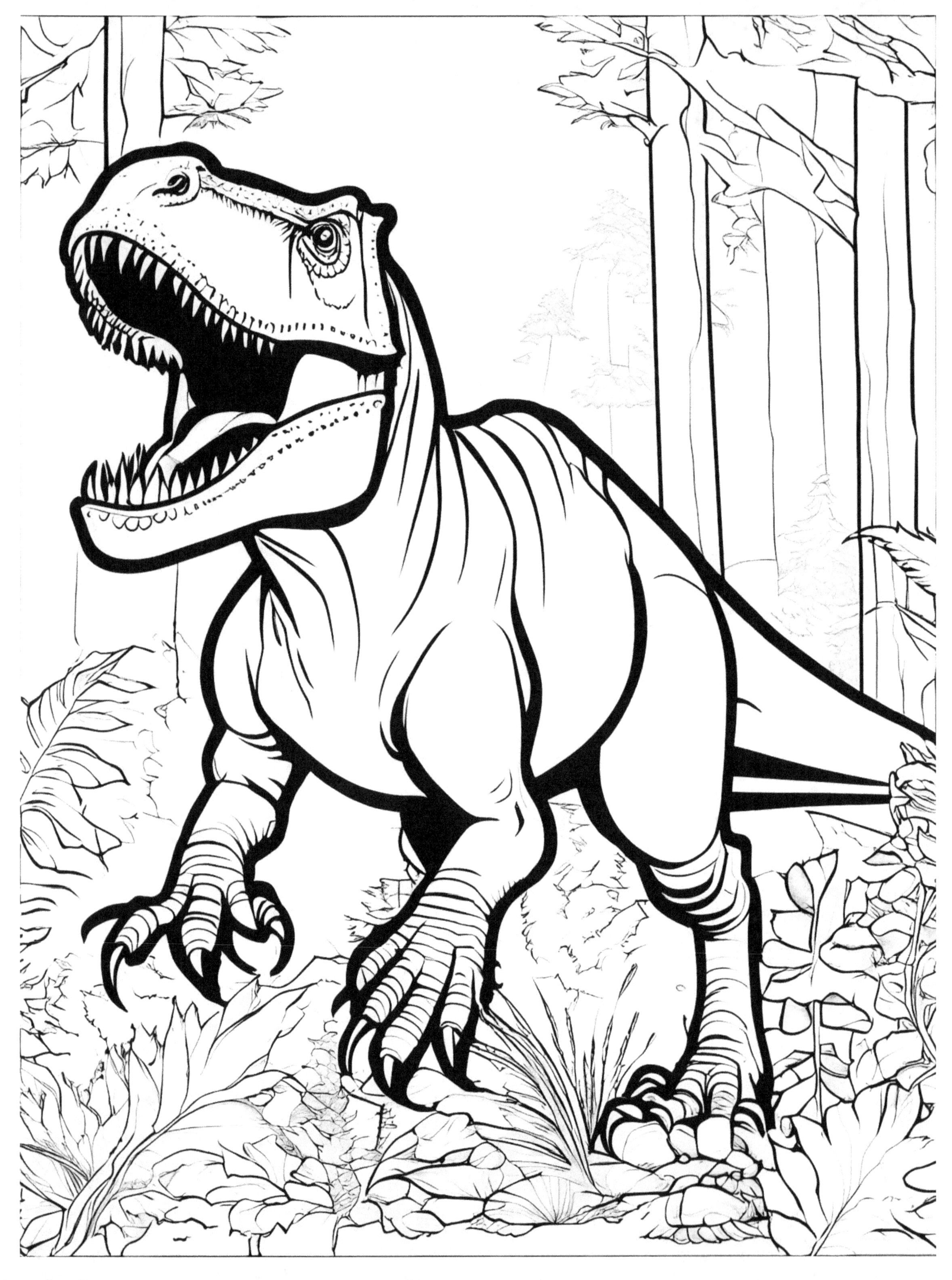

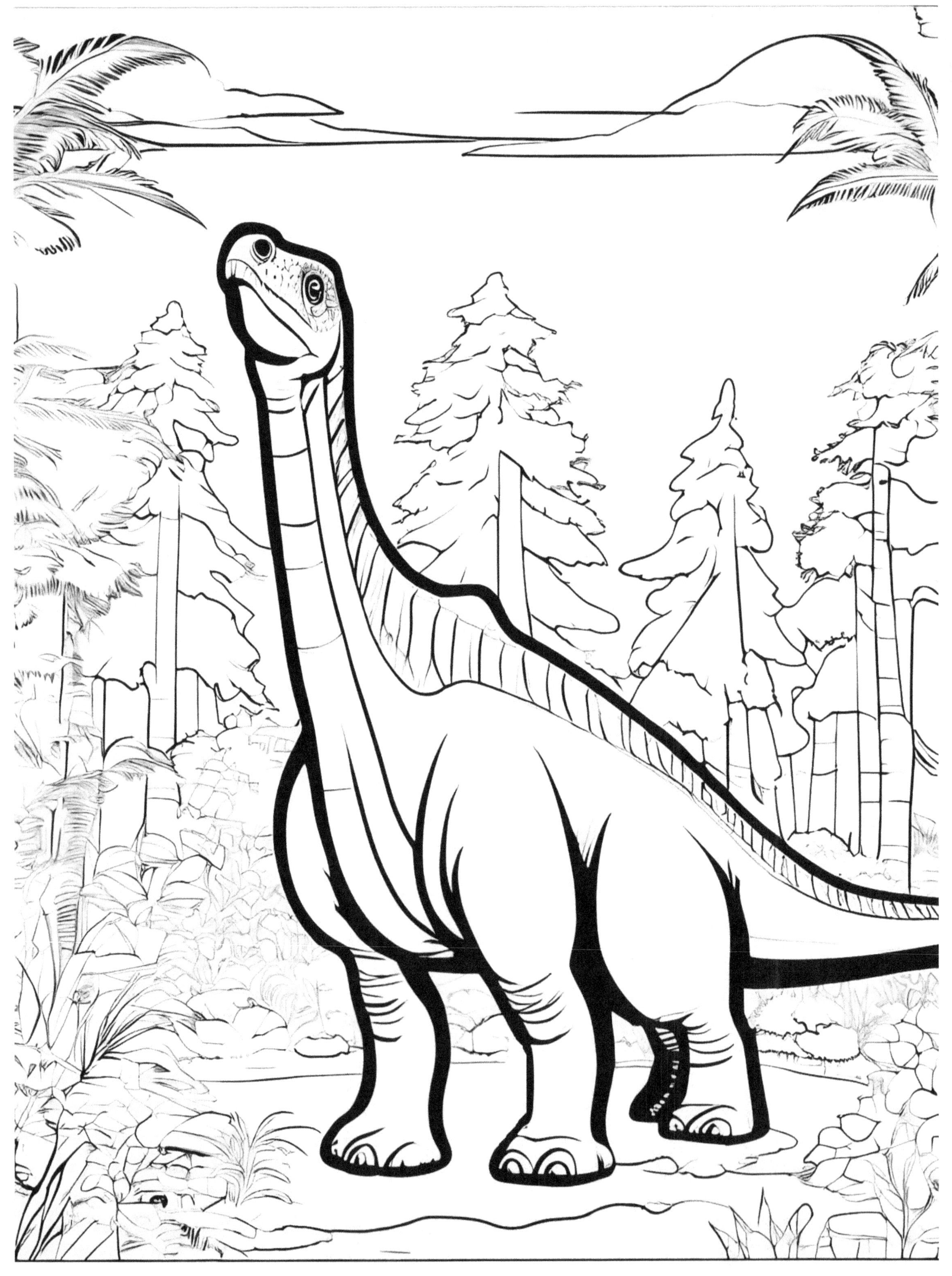

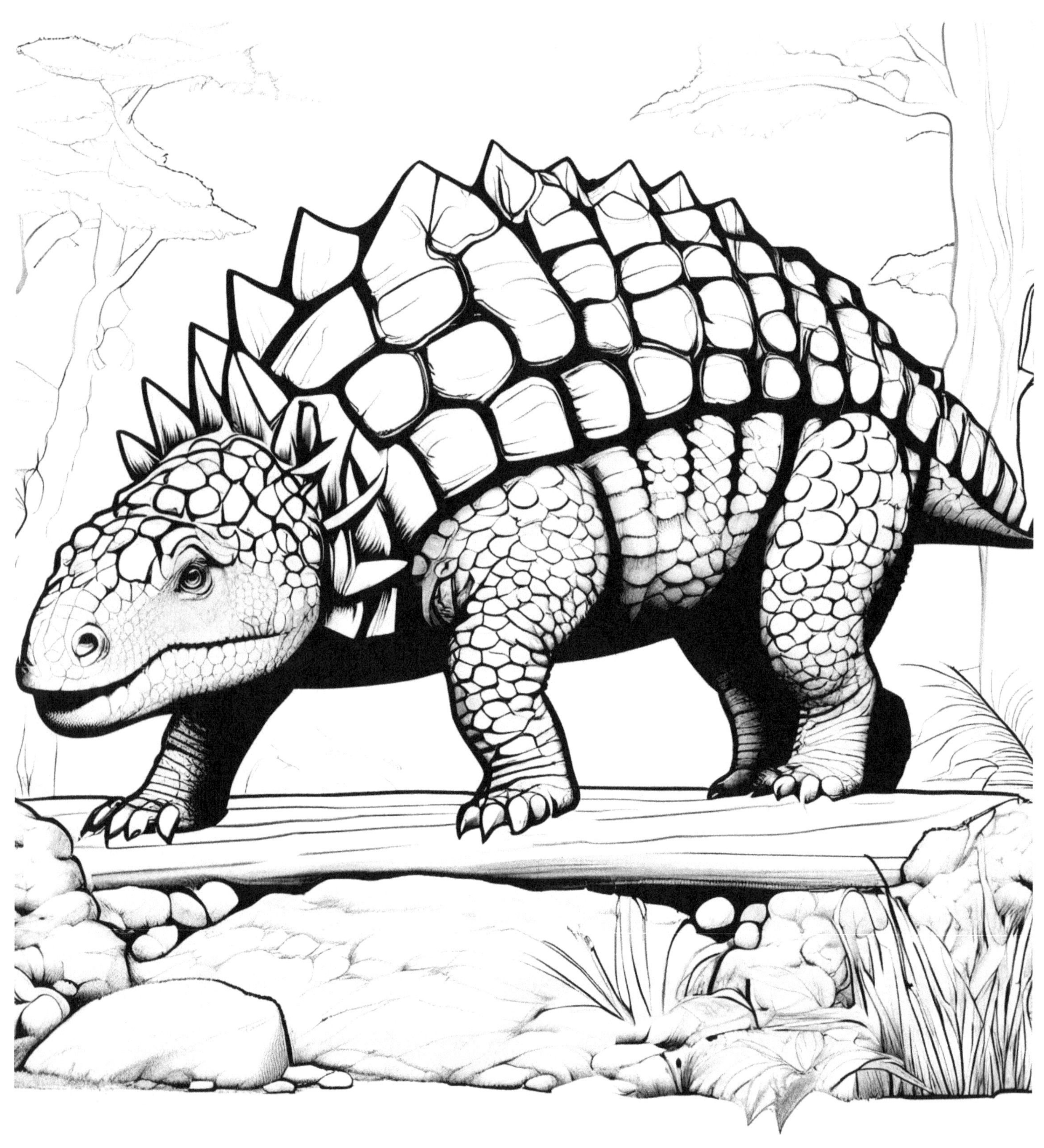

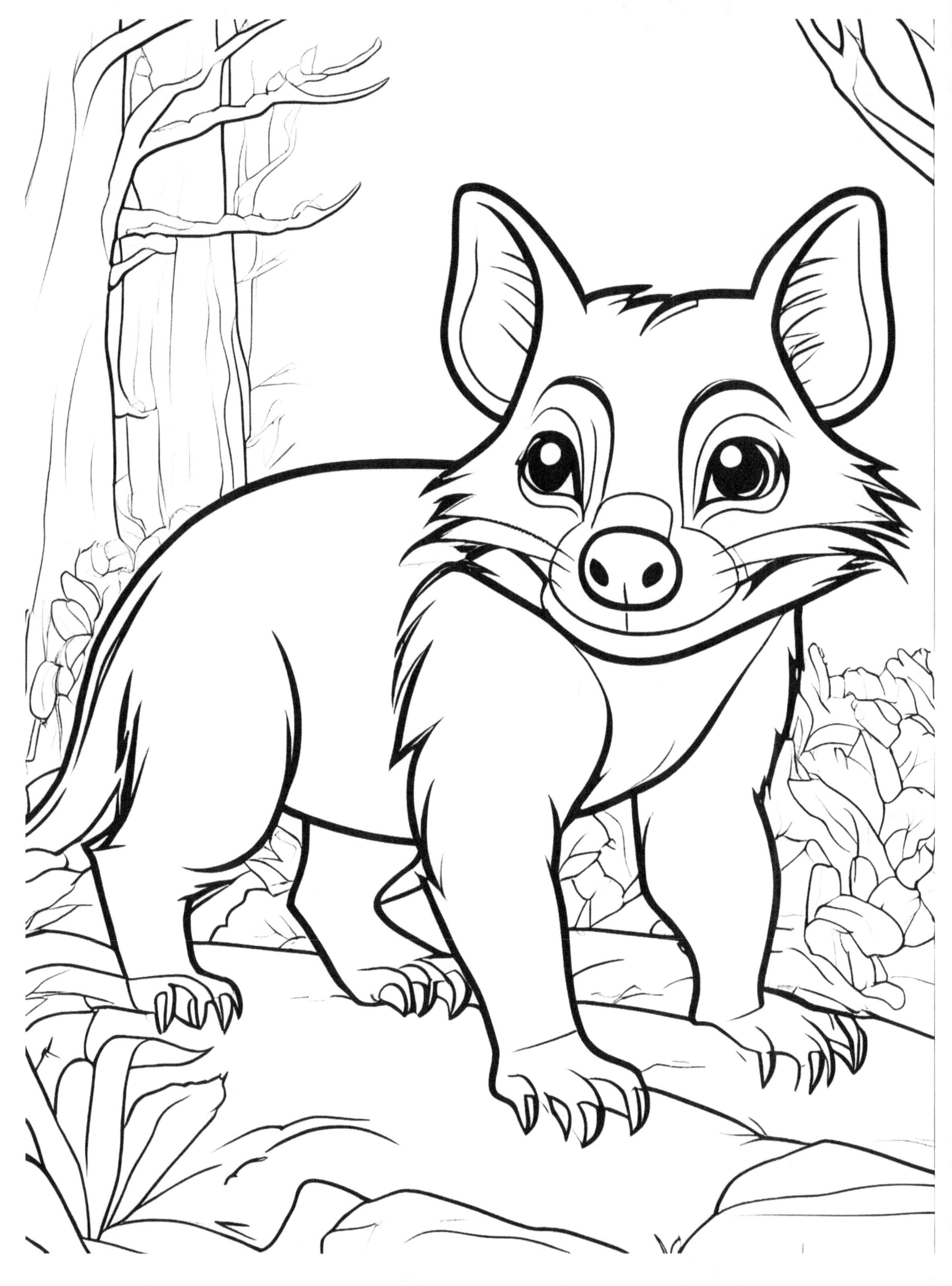

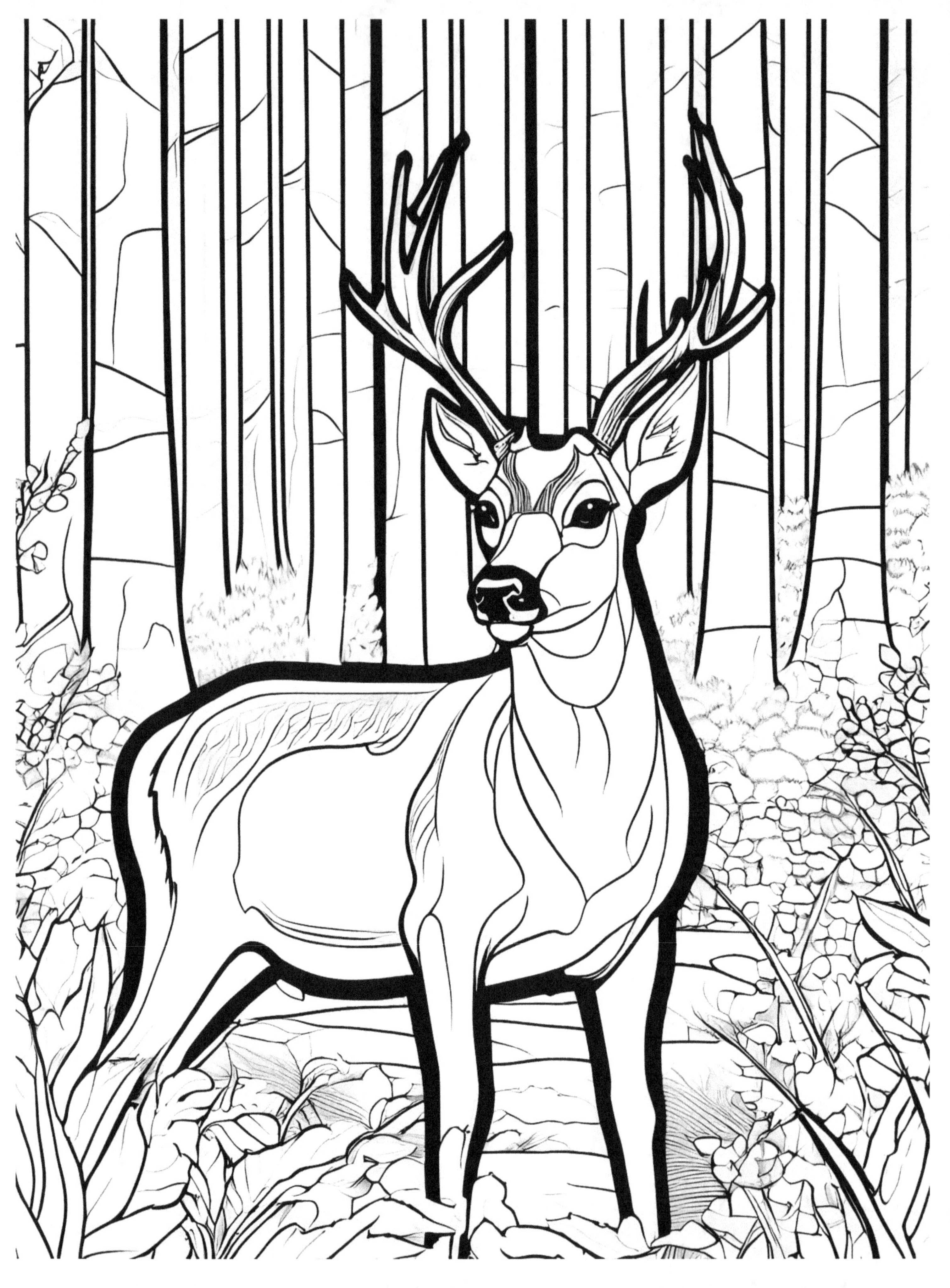